3-IN-1
JOKES, RIDDLES
&
TONGUE-TWISTERS
FOR KIDS

BY
ROB HILARIO

TABLE OF CONTENTS

PLEASE LEAVE A REVIEW

Knock-Knock!

I really hope your kids will enjoy this little book. And it would be great if you could take a moment of your time to jot down a short review on the book's Amazon Page. Your feedback is very important to me. It will also help others to make an informed decision before purchasing my book.

THANK YOU!

Rob Hilario

ANiMALS & PETS

Question: Why do kangaroo mums hate bad weather?

Answer: Their joeys have to play inside!

* * *

Q: What's small, furry and bright purple?

A: A koala holding its breath!

* * *

Q: What do you give an elephant with big feet?

A: Plenty of room!

* * *

Q: What happened to the cat that swallowed a ball of wool?

A: She had mittens!

* * *

Q: Why is there a crab in prison?

A: Because he kept pinching things!

* * *

Riddle!

What gets sharper the more you use it?

(Answer: page 62)

* * *

Q: Why the Teddy bears never feel hungry?

A: Because they are always stuffed!

* * *

Q: Why do hummingbirds hum?

A: Because they don't know the words!

* * *

Q: Why couldn't the leopard ever escape from the zoo?

A: He was always spotted.

* * *

Q: What a dog will do when he loses his tail?

A: He will prefer to go to a reTAIL store.

* * *

Q: Why are elephants so wrinkled?

A: Because it will take too long to iron an elephant!

* * *

Riddle!

What goes up and down, but still remains in

the same place?

(Answer: page 63)

* * *

Q: Why was the cat scared of the tree?

A: Because of its bark!

* * *

Q: What do you get when you cross an octopus and a cow?

A: An animal that can milk itself!

* * *

Q: What fur do we get from a Tiger?

A: As FUR away as possible!

* * *

Q: When is it bad luck to see a black cat?

A: When you're a mouse!

* * *

Q: Why is the barn so noisy?

A: Because the cows have horns!

* * *

Riddle!

Which one is correct? "Penguins flies" or "A Penguin flies"?

(Answer: page 64)

* * *

Q: What kind of key opens a banana?

A: A monkey.

* * *

Q: What do you call a cold dog?

A: chili dog!

* * *

Q: What steps will you take if a bear is running towards you?

A: Big ones!

* * *

Q: Why didn't the boy believe the tiger?

A: He thought it was a lion!

* * *

Q: What did the buffalo say to his son when he went away on a trip?

A: BiSON!

* * *

Riddle!

If it took eight men ten hours to build a wall, how long would it take four men to build it?

(Answer: page 65)

* * *

Q: What is 'out of bounds'?

A: An exhausted kangaroo!

* * *

Q: What do you get when you cross a snake and a pie?

A: A PIEthon!

* * *

Q: Why did the turkey cross the road?

A: To prove he wasn't chicken!

* * *

Q: Why did the lion spit out the clown?

A: Because he tasted funny!

* * *

Q: Why do penguins carry fish in their beaks?

A: Because they don't have any pockets!

* * *

Riddle!

If you are running in a race and you pass the person in second place, what place are you in?

(Answer: page 66)

* * *

Q: When is turkey soup bad for your health?

A: When you're the turkey!

* * *

Q: How does a lion greet the other animals in the field?

A: Pleased to eat you.

* * *

Q: How do porcupines kiss each other?

A: Very carefully!

* * *

Q: Why do gorillas have big nostrils?

A: Because they have big fingers!

* * *

Q: How do you fit more pigs on your farm?

A: Build a sty-scraper!

* * *

Riddle!

When you have me, you immediately feel like sharing me. But, if you do share me, you do not have me. What am I?

(Answer: page 67)

* * *

Q: Why do pandas like old movies?

A: Because they are black and white.

* * *

Q: What animal is best at baseball?

A: A bat!

* * *

Q: Why do cats make terrible storytellers?

A: They only have one tail.

* * *

Q: Where do they take squirrels when they go mad?

A: The nut house!

* * *

Q: What type of dog can tell the time?

A: A WATCHdog!

* * *

Q: What's a cat's favorite button on the tv remote?

A: Paws!

* * *

Riddle!

You are in a cabin and it is pitch black. You only have one match. Which do you light first, the newspaper, the lamp, the candle, or the fire?

(Answer: page 68)

SCHOOL & SCIENCE

Q: Why were the teacher's eyes crossed?

A: She couldn't control her pupils.

* * *

Q: What did the square say to the old circle?

A: Been around long?

* * *

Q: What's the difference between a teacher and a train?
A: Teacher says, "Spit out that gum!" and a train says, "Chew! Chew!"

* * *

Q: What is a math teacher's favorite sum?
A: Summer!

* * *

Q: What kind of school do you go to if you're a surfer?
A: Boarding school!

* * *

Riddle!
The more you take, the more you leave behind. What are they?
(Answer: page 69)

* * *

Q: What happened to the plant in math class?

A: It grew square roots.

* * *

Q: What do you call a music teacher with problems?

A: A trebled man.

* * *

Q: Why did the boy take a ladder to school?

A: Because he thought it was a HIGH school!

* * *

Q: Why was school much easier for cave people?

A: Because there was no history to study!

* * *

Q: What kind of food do math teachers eat?

A: Square meals!

* * *

Riddle!

Which is heavier: a pound of feathers or a
pound of rocks?

(Answer: page 70)

* * *

**Q: What do librarians take with them when
they go fishing?**

A: Bookworms!

* * *

Q: What building has the most stories?

A: The library!

* * *

**Q: Why did the student throw his watch out
of the school window?**

A: He wanted to see time fly.

* * *

Q: Why did the music teacher need a ladder?

17

A: To reach the high notes.

* * *

Q: Why do magicians do so well in school?
A: They're good at trick questions.

* * *

Riddle!
People buy me to eat, but never eat me.
What am I?
(Answer: page 71)

* * *

Q: What kind of school do you go to if you're an ice cream man?
A: Sundae school!

* * *

Q: What room can a student never enter?
A: A Mushroom.

* * *

Q: What letter is found in a cup?

A: T.

* * *

Q: What flies around the school at night?
A: The alpha-bat.

* * *

Q: Why did the Cyclops stop teaching?
A: Because he only had one pupil.

* * *

Riddle!

You draw a line. Without touching it, how do you make the line longer?

(Answer: page 72)

* * *

Q: Who is your best friend at school?
A: PrinciPAL.

* * *

Q: Why was the student's report card wet?
A: Because it was below C level.

* * *

Q: Why was the math book sad?

A: Because it had too many problems!

* * *

Q: What is the loudest state?

A: ILL-I-NOISE

* * *

Q: What is the smartest state?

A: Alabama, it has four A's and one B!

* * *

Riddle!

Which letter of the English alphabet flies, sings, and stings?

(Answer: page 73)

* * *

Q: Why was 6 afraid of 7?

A: Because 7 8 9.

* * *

Q: How do you spell Hard Water with 3 letters?

A: ICE!

* * *

Q: What is the Great Depression?

A: When you get a bad report card!

* * *

Q: Why did the teacher write the lesson on the windows?

A: He wanted the lesson to be very clear!

* * *

Q: What is further away, Australia or the Moon?

A: Australia. You can see the Moon at night!

* * *

Riddle!

You are my brother, but I am not your brother. Who am I?

21

(Answer: page 74)

* * *

Q: What would you get if you crossed a teacher and a vampire?

A: Lots of blood tests!

* * *

Q: Why didn't the sun go to college?

A: Because it already had a million degrees!

* * *

Q: Why did the teacher wear sunglasses?

A: Because her students were bright!

* * *

Q: Why was the music teacher not able to open his classroom?

A: Because his keys were on the piano.

* * *

Q: What's the best place to grow flowers in school?

A: In kindergarden.

* * *

Q: What is a snake's favorite subject?

A: HISStory!

* * *

Riddle!

Jimmy's mother had four children. She named the first Monday. She named the second Tuesday, and she named the third Wednesday. What is the name of the fourth child?

(Answer: page 75)

GHOSTS & MONSTERS

Q: What kind of ghost has the best hearing?

A: The eeriest.

* * *

Q: What do vampires take when they are sick?

A: Coffin drops!

* * *

Q: How can you tell a vampire likes baseball?

A: Every night he turns into a bat.

* * *

Q: What breed of dog does Dracula have?

A: A bloodhound!

* * *

Q: Why do witches fly on brooms?

A: Vacuum cleaner cords are too short.

* * *

Riddle!

What is full of holes but can still hold water?

(Answer: page 76)

* * *

Q: Why are vampires so easy to fool?

A: Because they are suckers.

* * *

Q: Why are ghosts bad liars?

A: You can see right through them.

* * *

Q: Do zombies eat dinner with their family?

A: No, their family IS the dinner!

* * *

Q: What kind of dessert do zombies like?

A: I-scream!

* * *

Q: Why didn't the skeleton eat spicy food?

A: He didn't have the stomach for it.

* * *

Riddle!

I have cities but no houses, oceans but without water, forests but no trees, deserts but no sand. What am I?

(Answer: page 77)

* * *

Q: What type of artist was the skeleton?
A: A SKULLptor.

* * *

Q: What happened when the werewolf went to the flea circus?
A: He stole the show!

* * *

Q: What do you get when you cross a werewolf with a hyena?
A: A creature with a sense of humor!

* * *

Q: What goes around a haunted house and never stops?
A: A fence!

* * *

Q: What happened to the skeleton who stayed by the fire for too long?

A: He became bone dry.

* * *

Riddle!

What flies when it's born, lies when it's alive, and runs when it's dead?

(Answer: page 78)

* * *

Q: Why doesn't Frankenstein go on airplanes?

A: He can't get past the airport metal detector.

* * *

Q: Where do ghosts mail letters?

A: The ghost office.

* * *

Q: What is vampire's favorite holiday?

A: FANGSgiving!

* * *

Q: When do ghosts usually appear?

A: Just before someone screams!

* * *

Q: Why was Frankenstein in jail?

A: He couldn't deny the charge.

* * *

Riddle!

A boy fell off a 100-foot ladder but did not get hurt. Why not?

(Answer: page 79)

* * *

Q: What's the problem with twin witches?

A: You can't tell which witch is which!

* * *

Q: What kind of music does a mummy listen to on his I-pod?

A: Wrap.

* * *

Q: What did the ghost say to another ghost?

A: Do you believe in humans?

* * *

Q: What's a zombie's favorite shampoo?

A: Head and shoulders!

* * *

Q: Do zombies eat popcorn with their fingers?

A: No, they eat their fingers separately.

* * *

Riddle!

What has hands but no feet, a face but no eyes, tells but doesn't talk?

(Answer: page 95)

* * *

Q: What do you do if you see zombies around your house?

A: Hope it is Halloween!

* * *

Q: Why couldn't the skeleton skydive?
A: He didn't have the guts.

* * *

Q: What do you call a zombie who keeps pressing your doorbell?
A: A DEAD ringer!

* * *

Q: Which musical instrument do skeletons play?
A: Trom-Bone!

* * *

Q: Why do ghosts only eat vegetables?
A: Because it's superNATURAL.

* * *

Riddle!
If an electric train is going east at 60 miles

31

an hour and there is a strong westerly wind, which way does the smoke from the train drift?

(Answer: page 80)

* * *

Q: Why does Frankenstein hurt so many people's feelings?
A: He's too Frank.

* * *

Q: What did the werewolf say to the flea?
A: Stop bugging me.

* * *

Q: Where do zombies live?
A: On dead end streets.

* * *

Q: Why did Dracula miss lunch?
A: Because he didn't fancy the stake.

* * *

Q: Why did Frankenstein's monster give up boxing?

A: Because he didn't want to spoil his looks.

* * *

Q: What does a skeleton order when he goes to a bar?

A: A beer and a mop.

* * *

Riddle!

Imagine that you are in a boat, in the middle of the sea. Suddenly, you are surrounded by hungry sharks, just waiting to feed on you. How can you put an end to this?

(Answer: page 81)

HOLIDAY SEASON

Q: What's a good time for Santa to come down the chimney?

A: Anytime!

* * *

Q: What are you giving Mom and Dad for Christmas?

A: A list of everything I want!

* * *

Q: What do you have in December that you don't have in any other month?

A: The letter "D"!

* * *

Q: What do snowmen like to do on the weekend?

A: Chill out.

* * *

Q: What's a good winter tip?

A: Never catch snowflakes with your tongue until all the birds have gone south for the winter.

* * *

Riddle!

Which hand is best for stirring sugar into a cup of tea?

(Answer: page 82)

* * *

Q: Why do we paint Easter eggs?

A: Because it's easier than trying to wallpaper them.

* * *

Q: Why don't aliens celebrate Christmas?

A: Because they don't want to give away their presence.

* * *

Q: Who is not hungry at Thanksgiving?

A: The turkey because he's already stuffed!

* * *

Q: What did Adam say the day before Christmas?

A: It's Christmas Eve.

* * *

Q: What did the snowman say to a kid?
A: Have an ice day!

* * *

Riddle!
What breaks and never falls and what falls and never breaks?
(Answer: page 83)

* * *

Q: Can February March?
A: No, but April May.

* * *

Q: How did Scrooge win the football game?
A: The ghost of Christmas PASSED.

* * *

Q: How do you know carrots are good for your eyes?

A: Have you ever seen an Easter Bunny wearing glasses?

* * *

Q: Which side of a turkey has the most feathers?
A: The outside!

* * *

Q: What's the difference between Santa's reindeer and a knight?
A: One slays the dragon, and the other's draggin' the sleigh.

* * *

Riddle!
What belongs to you but other people use it more than you?
(Answer: page 84)

* * *

Q: Why are Christmas trees so bad at

sewing?

A: They always drop their needles!

* * *

Q: What nationality is Santa Claus?

A: North Polish!

* * *

Q: Why did the farmer wear one boot to town?

A: Because he heard there would be a 50% chance of snow!

* * *

Q: What's the key to a great Thanksgiving dinner?

A: The turKEY.

* * *

Q: Why do pumpkins sit on people's porches?

A: They have no hands to knock on the door.

* * *

Riddle!

How can a man go 8 days without sleep?

(Answer: page 85)

* * *

Q: Which of Santa's reindeer has bad manners?

A: RUDEolph.

* * *

Q: Where did Santa find the elf?

A: On the shelf.

* * *

Q: What do Thanksgiving and Halloween have in common?

A: One has gobblers, the other has goblins.

* * *

Q: What is a pumpkin's favorite sport?

A: Squash!

* * *

Q: Why did the Pilgrims eat turkey at Thanksgiving?

A: Because they couldn't fit the moose in the oven!

* * *

Riddle!

How can you throw a ball as hard as you can, to only have it come back to you, even if it doesn't bounce off anything?

(Answer: page 86)

* * *

Q: Why did the Easter egg hide?

A: He was a little chicken!

* * *

Q: What kind of ball doesn't bounce?

A: A snowball!

* * *

Q: Who is Frosty's favorite Aunt?

A: Aunt Arctica!

* * *

Q: What do you call a snowman in the desert?

A: A puddle!

* * *

Q: What sorts of cakes do snowmen like best?

A: Ones with thick icing.

* * *

Riddle!

20 pigeons sat on the branches of a tree. A man shot 1 pigeon with his gun. How many were left on the tree?

(Answer: page 87)

* * *

Q: Why does Santa go down the chimney on

Christmas?

A: Because it soots him!

* * *

Q: Why don't mountains get cold in the winter?

A: They wear snow caps.

* * *

Q: Why was the snowman's dog called Frost?

A: Because Frost bites!

* * *

Q: Why does Santa ride a sleigh?

A: It's too heavy to carry!

LITTLE OF EVERYTHING

Q: What do you call a boomerang that doesn't come back?

A: A stick!

* * *

Q: Why did the man throw the butter out the window?

A: Because he wanted to see BUTTERfly.

* * *

Q: What did one eye say to the other?

A: Between you and me something smells.

* * *

Q: What kind of a star can be dangerous?

A: A shooting star!

* * *

Q: Why did the runner stop listening to music?

A: Because she broke too many records.

* * *

Riddle!

If there are 6 apples and you take away 4, how many do you have?

(Answer: page 88)

* * *

Q: What is the color of the wind?

A: Blew.

* * *

Q: Why did the banana go to the doctor?

A: Because he wasn't peeling very well!

* * *

Q: What kind of button can you not undo?

A: A belly button!

* * *

Q: What kind of nut has no shell?

A: A doughNUT!

* * *

Q: Why did the farmer bury all his money?

A: To make his soil rich!

* * *

Riddle!

What two words, when combined hold the most letters?

(Answer: page 89)

* * *

Q: What does an envelope say when you lick it?

A: Nothing. It just shuts up.

* * *

Q: How do athletes stay cool during a game?

A: They sit near the fans!

* * *

Q: How did the ocean say goodbye?

A: It waved!

* * *

Q: Why can't you trust atoms?

A: They make up everything!

* * *

Q: What gives you the power and strength to walk through walls?

A: A door!

* * *

Riddle!

I exist only when there is light, but direct light kills me. What am I?

(Answer: page 90)

* * *

Q: Why does your nose run?

A: Because it can't walk!

* * *

Q: Why did the bubble gum cross the road?

A: It was stuck to the dog's foot!

* * *

Q: How much room is needed for fungi to grow?

A: As mushroom as possible!

* * *

Q: What did the tree say after a long winter?
A: What a re-leaf!

* * *

Q: What happens when you wear a snowsuit inside?
A: It melts!

* * *

Riddle!
I'm lighter than a feather, yet the strongest man can't hold me for more than 5 minutes. What am I?
(Answer: page 91)

* * *

Q: What is the best thing to put into a pie?
A: A fork!

* * *

Q: What kind of fish is famous?

A: A STARfish!

* * *

Q: Which runs faster, hot or cold?

A: Hot. Everyone can catch a cold.

* * *

Q: Which are the stronger days of the week?

A: Saturday and Sunday. The rest are WEAKdays.

* * *

Q: What did the baby corn say to a mama corn?

A: Where is POPcorn?

* * *

Riddle!

I do not have any special powers, but I can predict the score of any football game before it begins. How can I do this?

(Answer: page 92)

* * *

Q: How do you make an egg roll?

A: You push it.

* * *

Q: Do you serve chicken here?

A: Sit down, sir. We serve anyone.

* * *

Q: What did the picture say to the wall?

A: I was framed!

* * *

Q: What did one candle say to the other candle?

A: Are you going out tonight?

* * *

Q: What did the blanket say to the bed?

A: Don't worry. I got you covered.

* * *

Riddle!

In a year, there are 12 months. Seven months have 31 days. How many months have 28 days?

(Answer: page 93)

* * *

Q: Where are cars most likely to get flat tires?

A: At forks in the road.

* * *

Q: What can you put in a barrel to make it lighter?

A: Holes!

* * *

Q: Why did the thief take a shower?

A: He wanted to make a clean getaway!

* * *

Q: Why did the melon jump into the lake?

A: It wanted to be a watermelon.

* * *

Q: Why was the boy sitting on his watch?

A: Because he wanted to be on time.

* * *

Riddle!

What has a head and a tail but no body?

(Answer: page 94)

TONGUE-TWISTERS

Black bug's blood (repeat 3 times)

* * *

Twelve twins twirled twelve twigs.

* * *

Seven slick slimy snakes slowly sliding southward.

* * *

Gertie's great-grandma grew aghast at Gertie's grammar.

* * *

Susie works in a shoeshine shop. Where she shines she sits, and where she sits she shines.

* * *

How many cans can a canner can, if a canner can can cans?
A canner can can as many cans as a canner can, if a canner can can cans.

* * *

She sells seashells by the seashore.
The shells she sells are surely seashells.
So if she sells shells on the seashore
I'm sure she sells seashore shells.

Six sticky skeletons (repeat 3 times)

* * *

Clowns grow glowing crowns.

* * *

A big bug bit the little beetle but the little beetle bit the big bug back.

* * *

Betty bought butter but the butter was bitter, so Betty bought better butter to make the bitter butter better.

* * *

Firefighters found Father frowning from a funny fever and farting fierce flames.

* * *

The sixth sick sheik's sixth sheep is sick.

* * *

If colored caterpillars could change their colors constantly could they keep their colored coat colored properly?

* * *

If Freaky Fred Found Fifty Feet of Fruit And Fed Forty Feet to his Friend Frank How many Feet of Fruit did Freaky Fred Find?

She sees cheese (repeat 3 times)

* * *

I saw Susie sitting in a shoe shine shop.

* * *

Each Easter Eddie eats eighty Easter eggs.

* * *

If a dog chews shoes, whose shoes does he choose?

* * *

A big black bug bit a big black bear, but the big black bear bit the big black bug back.

* * *

If eight great apes ate eighty-eight grapes, guess how many grapes each great ape ate?

* * *

Rory the warrior and Roger the worrier were reared wrongly in a rural brewery.

* * *

I wish to wish the wish you wish to wish, but if you wish the wish the witch wishes, I won't wish the wish you wish to wish.

Black back bat (repeat 3 times)

* * *

Five frantic frogs fled from fifty fierce fishes.

* * *

Two tiny timid toads trying to trot to Tarrytown.

* * *

No need to light a night-light on a light night like tonight.

* * *

Three thin thinkers thinking thick
thoughtful thoughts.

* * *

If two witches would watch two watches,
which witch would watch which watch?

* * *

How much caramel can a canny cannonball
cram in a camel
if a canny cannonball can cram caramel in a
camel?

* * *

How many cookies could a good cook
if a good cook could cook cookies?
A good cook could cook as many cookies
as a good cook who could cook cookies.

Thin sticks, thick bricks (repeat 3 times)

* * *

Growing gray goats graze great green grassy groves.

* * *

Lesser leather never weathered wetter weather better.

* * *

The big, bumbling bear burned his butt baking bread.

* * *

Nine nimble noblemen nibbling nuts.

* * *

Round the rough and rugged rock, the ragged rascal rudely ran.

* * *

He thrusts his fists against the posts and still insists he sees the ghosts.

* * *

A skunk sat on a stump.

The stump thought the skunk stunk.

The skunk thought the stump stunk.

What stunk, the skunk or the stump?

ANSWERS TO RIDDLES

YOUR BRAIN!

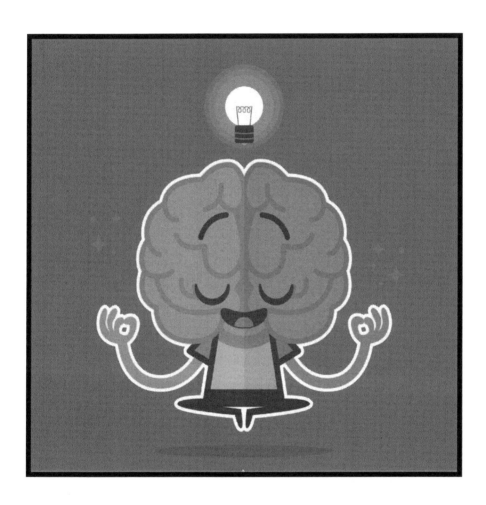

STAIRS!

NEITHER.
PENGUINS DON'T FLY.

NO TIME AT ALL.
IT IS ALREADY BUILT.

SECOND PLACE

A Secret

YOU LIGHT THE MATCH FIRST!

FOOTPRINTS

NEITHER.
BOTH WEIGH A POUND!

PLATE

YOU DRAW A SHORTER LINE NEXT TO iT.
AND iT BECOMES THE LONGER LINE.

'B' (BEE)

i AM YOUR SiSTER!

JiMMY.
BECAUSE JiMMY'S MOTHER HAD FOUR CHILDREN!

A SPONGE

A MAP

SNOWFLAKE

HE FELL OFF THE BOTTOM STEP

THERE IS NO SMOKE COMING FROM ELECTRIC TRAINS

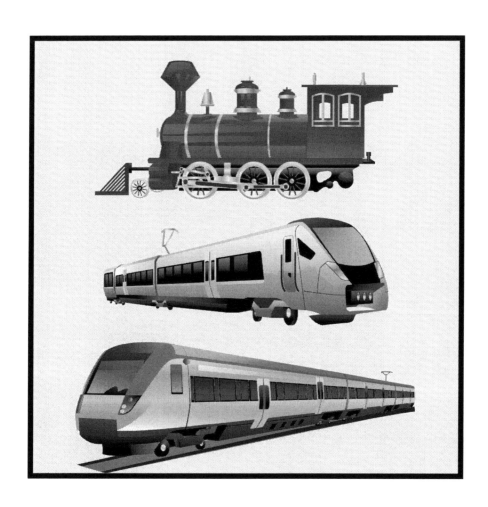

STOP IMAGINING!

IT'S BETTER TO USE A SPOON

DAY BREAKS, NIGHT FALLS

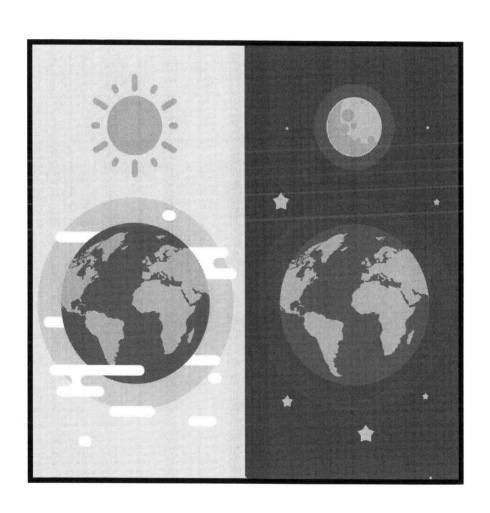

YOUR NAME

HE SLEEPS AT NIGHT

THROW THE BALL STRAIGHT UP IN THE AIR

NONE.
THE REST FLEW AWAY.

THE FOUR APPLES YOU TOOK!

POST OFFICE

SHADOW

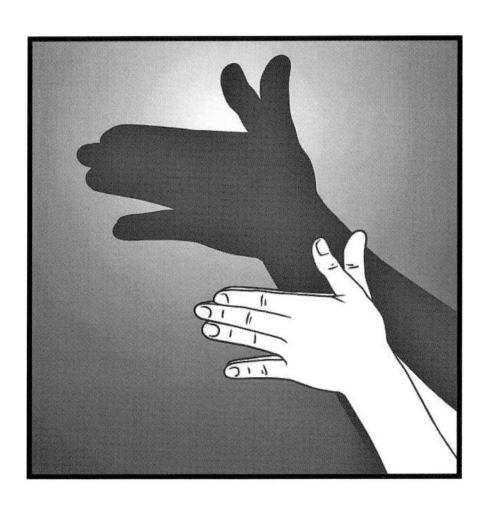

BREATH

THE SCORE BEFORE ANY FOOTBALL GAME IS ALWAYS ZERO TO ZERO!

EVERY MONTH HAS AT LEAST 28 DAYS

A COiN

A CLOCK

PLEASE LEAVE A REVIEW

Knock-Knock!

I hope your kids have enjoyed reading this little book. And it would be great if you could take a moment of your time to jot down a short review on the book's Amazon Page. Your feedback is very important to me. It will also help others to make an informed decision before purchasing my book.

THANK YOU!

Rob Hilario

CREDITS

All images designed by: Freepik, Dooder / Freepik, Visnezh / Freepik, Frimufilms / Freepik, ddraw / Freepik, Photoroyalty / Freepik, Euco / Freepik, Graphiqastock / Freepik, iconicbestiary / Freepik, Kreativkolors / Freepik.

97823432R00055

Made in the USA
Middletown, DE
07 November 2018